MAKING MONEY ONLINE: BOOK 9

BY MICHAEL CALLUM MAYAKA

ONLINE CONSULTING AND COACHING

FOREWORD:

In today's digital age, making money online has become a viable and accessible option for individuals seeking financial independence or additional income streams. The internet offers a plethora of opportunities that allow you to leverage your skills, creativity, and resources to generate revenue. This guide aims to provide you with valuable insights, strategies, and practical tips on how to make money online effectively.

This book is part of a series for more information see Further reading at the end of this book.

Table of Contents

Foreword: 3

9. Online Consulting and Coaching 5

    9.1 Consulting Services and Expertise: Leveraging Knowledge for Online Income 6

        Introduction: 6

        The Value of Consulting Services: 7

        Identifying Your Consulting Niche: 8

        Building Credibility and Expertise: 9

        Finding Clients and Marketing Your Services: 10

        Delivering Value and Building Relationships: 12

        Conclusion: 14

    9.2 Life Coaching and Personal Development 15

        Introduction: 15

        Understanding Life Coaching: 16

        Benefits of Life Coaching: 16

        Personal Development and Growth: 19

        Conclusion: 23

    9.3 Health and Fitness Coaching 24

        Introduction: 24

        The Role of Health and Fitness Coaching: 25

        Benefits of Health and Fitness Coaching: 26

        Impact of Health and Fitness Coaching: 29

        Conclusion: 31

Further reading: 33

9. ONLINE CONSULTING AND COACHING

9.1 CONSULTING SERVICES AND EXPERTISE: LEVERAGING KNOWLEDGE FOR ONLINE INCOME

INTRODUCTION:

Consulting services provide a valuable opportunity to monetize your expertise and knowledge. Whether you possess industry-specific insights, technical skills, or specialized experience, offering consulting services online allows you to assist individuals and businesses while generating income. In this section, we will explore the world of online consulting, including its benefits, key considerations, and effective strategies for success.

THE VALUE OF CONSULTING SERVICES:

Consulting services bridge the gap between those seeking guidance and those with expert knowledge. Businesses and individuals often require professional advice to solve complex problems, optimize operations, or strategize for growth. By offering consulting services, you position yourself as an authority in your field and can provide valuable insights and recommendations that can drive tangible results.

IDENTIFYING YOUR CONSULTING NICHE:

To succeed as an online consultant, it's crucial to identify and define your consulting niche. Consider your expertise, skills, and experience, and align them with the needs and demands of your target market. This clarity allows you to position yourself as a specialist and attract clients who value your specific knowledge and insights. Narrowing down your niche also helps differentiate you from competitors and establish a unique selling proposition.

BUILDING CREDIBILITY AND EXPERTISE:

Establishing credibility and demonstrating your expertise are essential for attracting clients and building trust. Here are a few strategies to enhance your online presence and establish yourself as a trusted consultant:

1. Develop a professional website or portfolio showcasing your qualifications, achievements, and client testimonials.

2. Create high-quality content such as blog posts, articles, or videos that showcase your knowledge and provide value to your target audience.

3. Engage in social media platforms and online communities related to your industry,

sharing insights and participating in discussions.

4. Offer free resources, such as e-books or webinars, to establish yourself as a thought leader in your field.

FINDING CLIENTS AND MARKETING YOUR SERVICES:

To find clients as an online consultant, you need to adopt effective marketing strategies. Here are some approaches to consider:

1. Network within your industry and attend relevant conferences or events to connect with potential clients.

2. Leverage social media platforms, online forums, and professional networking sites to reach your target audience.

3. Utilize search engine optimization (SEO) techniques to improve your visibility in online searches.

4. Collaborate with complementary professionals or businesses to expand your reach through partnerships or referrals.

5. Offer introductory or discounted rates for initial clients to build your portfolio and gain referrals and positive testimonials.

DELIVERING VALUE AND BUILDING RELATIONSHIPS:

Providing exceptional value and building strong relationships with your clients are crucial for long-term success. Some key considerations include:

1. Understand your clients' specific needs and tailor your consulting services accordingly.

2. Conduct thorough research and analysis to provide well-informed recommendations and solutions.

3. Maintain open and effective communication channels to address any concerns or questions promptly.

4. Continuously update your knowledge and skills to stay at the forefront of your industry and provide the best possible value to your clients.

5. Seek feedback from clients to understand their satisfaction levels and identify areas for improvement.

CONCLUSION:

Online consulting services offer a lucrative avenue to monetize your expertise and provide valuable guidance to clients in need. By identifying your consulting niche, establishing credibility, effectively marketing your services, and delivering exceptional value, you can build a successful consulting practice online. Remember, success as a consultant relies on continuous learning, adaptability, and a client-centric approach. With dedication and the right strategies, you can thrive in the online consulting world and create a fulfilling and profitable career.

9.2 LIFE COACHING AND PERSONAL DEVELOPMENT

INTRODUCTION:

Life coaching and personal development have gained significant popularity in recent years as people increasingly seek guidance and support in achieving their goals, overcoming challenges, and finding fulfilment in their lives. This article explores the concept of life coaching, its benefits, and how personal development plays a crucial role in empowering individuals to unlock their full potential and lead more meaningful lives.

UNDERSTANDING LIFE COACHING:

Life coaching is a collaborative partnership between a trained professional, known as a life coach, and a client. The coach helps the client identify their goals, aspirations, and areas for improvement, and then guides them through a process of self-discovery and personal growth. The focus is on assisting individuals in bridging the gap between where they currently are in life and where they desire to be.

BENEFITS OF LIFE COACHING:

1. Clarity and Goal Setting: A life coach helps clients gain clarity about their values,

passions, and purpose in life. Through meaningful conversations and exercises, individuals can define their goals more effectively, establish action plans, and stay focused on achieving them.

2. Accountability and Motivation: Life coaching provides a supportive and accountable environment where individuals are encouraged to take consistent action towards their goals. Coaches help clients stay motivated, overcome obstacles, and maintain momentum in their personal growth journey.

3. Personal Empowerment: Life coaching empowers individuals to take ownership of

their lives. It promotes self-awareness, boosts self-confidence, and enhances decision-making abilities. Clients learn to identify and leverage their strengths while addressing areas that require improvement.

4. Improved Relationships: Life coaching explores the dynamics of personal and professional relationships. Clients gain insights into effective communication, conflict resolution, and creating healthy boundaries. This leads to more fulfilling connections with others and greater satisfaction in personal interactions.

5. Stress Management and Work-Life Balance: Life coaching addresses the

challenges of stress, burnout, and maintaining a healthy work-life balance. Coaches assist clients in developing strategies to manage stress, prioritize self-care, and create harmony between personal and professional spheres.

PERSONAL DEVELOPMENT AND GROWTH:

Personal development refers to the lifelong process of self-improvement, learning, and growth. It involves developing new skills, expanding knowledge, and nurturing positive habits and mindsets. Personal development encompasses various aspects, including:

1. Self-Awareness: Understanding one's strengths, weaknesses, values, and beliefs is crucial for personal growth. Self-reflection, mindfulness practices, and feedback from others help individuals gain deeper insights into themselves.

2. Continuous Learning: Personal development involves embracing a growth mindset and seeking opportunities for learning and skill development. This can be achieved through reading, attending seminars, taking courses, or acquiring new experiences.

3. Emotional Intelligence: Developing emotional intelligence allows individuals to

understand and manage their emotions effectively. It involves empathy, self-regulation, social skills, and increased awareness of one's emotional triggers.

4. Healthy Habits: Personal development promotes the cultivation of positive habits such as regular exercise, proper nutrition, adequate sleep, and stress reduction techniques. These habits contribute to overall well-being and enhance productivity.

5. Self-Care: Prioritizing self-care is essential for personal development. This includes setting boundaries, practicing self-compassion, engaging in activities that bring

joy and relaxation, and maintaining a healthy work-life balance.

CONCLUSION:

Life coaching and personal development provide individuals with the tools, guidance, and support necessary for personal growth and fulfilment. Through life coaching, individuals can set clear goals, overcome obstacles, and achieve their desired outcomes. Personal development empowers individuals to continuously learn, evolve, and embrace a holistic approach to self-improvement. By investing in their personal growth, individuals can lead more purposeful lives, create meaningful relationships, and unlock their full potential.

9.3 HEALTH AND FITNESS COACHING

INTRODUCTION:

In today's fast-paced world, health and fitness have become increasingly important for individuals striving to maintain a balanced and fulfilling lifestyle. Health and fitness coaching has emerged as a valuable profession that helps individuals achieve their wellness goals through personalized guidance, education, and motivation. This article explores the role of health and fitness coaching, the benefits it offers, and how it can positively impact people's lives.

THE ROLE OF HEALTH AND FITNESS COACHING:

Health and fitness coaching involves working closely with individuals to help them develop and maintain healthy habits, make sustainable lifestyle changes, and achieve their wellness objectives. Coaches provide personalized guidance based on an individual's unique needs, preferences, and circumstances. They serve as a trusted mentor, offering support, accountability, and expert knowledge to empower clients on their health and fitness journeys.

BENEFITS OF HEALTH AND FITNESS COACHING:

1. Personalized Approach: Health and fitness coaching takes into account an individual's specific goals, challenges, and preferences. Coaches tailor programs and strategies to suit each client, providing personalized guidance that maximizes the chances of success.

2. Goal Setting and Accountability: Coaches assist clients in setting realistic, achievable goals and create action plans to reach them. They provide ongoing support and hold clients accountable, helping them stay motivated, focused, and consistent in their efforts.

3. Education and Empowerment: Health and fitness coaches offer valuable education and information regarding nutrition, exercise, stress management, and overall well-being. They empower clients by equipping them with the knowledge and tools necessary to make informed decisions about their health.

4. Lifestyle Modification: One of the primary focuses of health and fitness coaching is to promote lasting lifestyle changes. Coaches help clients identify and overcome barriers to change, establish healthy habits, and integrate them seamlessly into their daily lives.

5. Motivation and Support: Staying motivated can be challenging, especially when faced with obstacles or setbacks. Health and fitness coaches provide ongoing encouragement, support, and guidance, helping clients overcome obstacles and maintain their motivation during challenging times.

6. Holistic Approach: Health and fitness coaching recognizes that optimal well-being extends beyond just physical fitness. Coaches take a holistic approach, addressing various aspects of a person's life, including nutrition, exercise, sleep, stress management, and emotional well-being.

IMPACT OF HEALTH AND FITNESS COACHING:

Health and fitness coaching can have a profound impact on individuals' lives by promoting positive lifestyle changes and improving overall well-being. Some of the key impacts include:

1. Enhanced Physical Fitness: Health and fitness coaching can help individuals improve their physical fitness levels, increase strength, flexibility, and cardiovascular health through personalized exercise programs.

2. Weight Management: Coaches assist clients in setting realistic weight management goals and developing sustainable strategies to achieve them. They provide guidance on healthy eating habits, portion control, and mindful eating practices.

3. Improved Nutrition: Health and fitness coaches educate clients about balanced nutrition, helping them make healthier food choices, develop meal plans, and understand the role of nutrition in overall health.

4. Stress Reduction: Through stress management techniques, such as mindfulness, relaxation exercises, and

lifestyle adjustments, coaches help individuals reduce stress levels, enhance resilience, and improve mental well-being.

5. Increased Confidence and Self-Esteem: Achieving health and fitness goals can significantly boost confidence and self-esteem. Coaches provide the support and encouragement necessary for clients to believe in themselves and their ability to make positive changes.

CONCLUSION:

Health and fitness coaching plays a vital role in empowering individuals to take control of their well-being. By providing personalized guidance, education, and support, coaches help clients make sustainable lifestyle changes that lead to improved physical fitness, mental well-being, and overall quality of life. Whether the goal is weight loss, stress reduction, or long-term health maintenance.

FURTHER READING:

If you enjoyed this book, please consider reading one of the other books in the series:

Making Money Online: Book 1 (Understanding the Online Landscape)

Making Money Online: Book 2 (E-commerce and Online Retail)

Making Money Online: Book 3 (Freelancing and Remote Work)

Making Money Online: Book 4 (Content Creation and Monetization)

Making Money Online: Book 5 (Online Tutoring and Education)

Making Money Online: Book 6 (Online Surveys, Microtasks, and Rewards)

Making Money Online: Book 7 (Online Investments and Trading)

Making Money Online: Book 8 (Creating and Selling Digital Assets)

Making Money Online: Book 9 (Online Consulting and Coaching)

Making Money Online: Book 10 (Maximizing Online Income Opportunities)

All the books can be found on Amazon as Kindle and Paperback, or you can buy the complete edition which contains the full series in one book. The complete edition is available as Kindle, Paperback and exclusively as Hardback. You can find all the links in my book site: books.michaelmayaka.co.uk.

www.ingramcontent.com/pod-product-compliance
Lightning Source LLC
Chambersburg PA
CBHW040300220526
45473CB00002B/538